INNSBRUCK TRAVEL GUIDE 2024 -2025

Discover the Heart of the Austrian Alps

Alfred M. Pfeiffer

A footbridge crosses the Sill River in Innsbruck, Austria, with a cyclist nearing the bridge.

Large groups of people, including both locals and tourists, wander through the numerous shops, cafes, and restaurants in Innsbruck's spacious Market Square Plaza.

Table Of Content

Five European Cities Close to Innsbruck

Munich, Germany to Innsbruck by Car: approximately 165 km

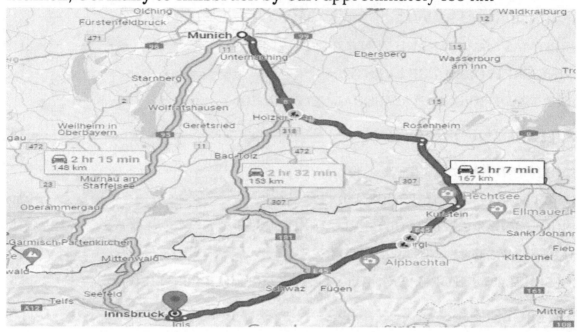

Salzburg, Austria to Innsbruck by Car: approximately 185 km

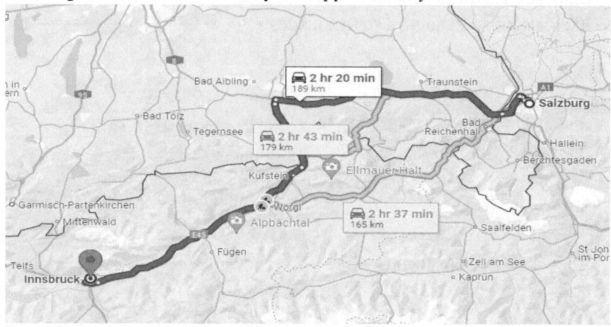

Zurich, Switzerland to Innsbruck by Car: approximately 285 km

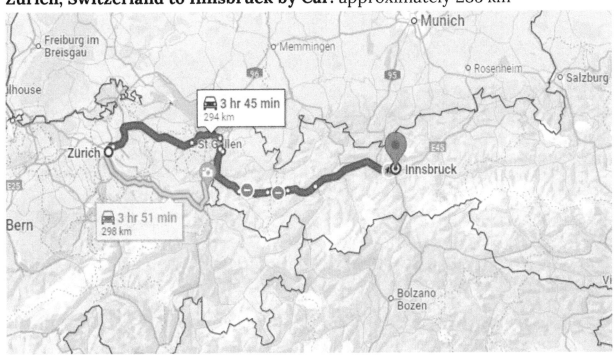

Bolzano, Italy, to Innsbruck by Car:

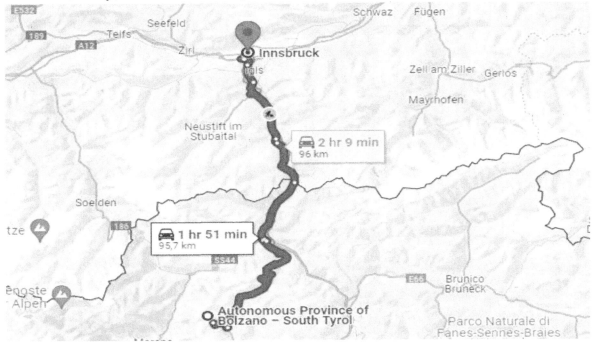

Vaduz, Liechtenstein to Innsbruck By Car: approximately 180 km

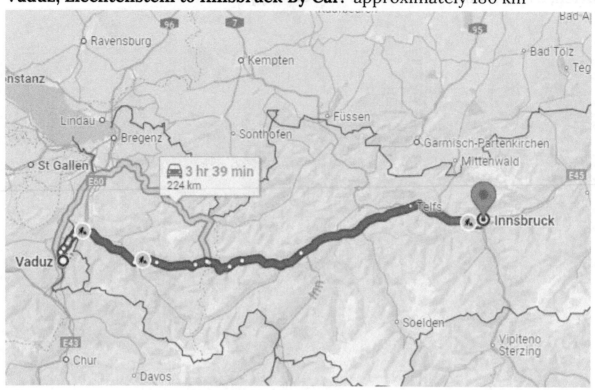

Introduction

Welcome to Innsbruck

Situated in the heart of the Austrian Alps, Innsbruck is a place where stunning natural landscapes intersect with rich historical charm. As the capital of Tyrol, Innsbruck has long been a magnet for adventure enthusiasts, history buffs, and culture aficionados. Framed by snow-dusted peaks, this alpine gem offers a multitude of activities that appeal to every type of traveler, from exploring ancient architecture to partaking in world-class skiing adventures.

Innsbruck boasts a vibrant blend of history, art, and culture that is sure to captivate and inspire visitors. This guide is designed to accompany you as you wander through its cobblestone lanes, lively districts, and magnificent vistas. Whether you are visiting for the first time or are a returning traveler, Innsbruck has something unique for everyone.

How to Use This Guide

This travel guide is crafted to help you maximize your time in Innsbruck, providing valuable insights and practical advice to ensure a smooth and enjoyable visit. Here's how to utilize this guide effectively:

- **Detailed Sections:** Each chapter is structured to deliver in-depth information on specific facets of Innsbruck, from uncovering historical landmarks to exploring hidden treasures. Use the table of contents to easily navigate to topics of interest.
- **Practical Tips:** Throughout the guide, you will find useful tips on everything from local customs and transportation options to dining suggestions and safety guidelines. These insights are designed to help you navigate like a local and steer clear of typical tourist traps.

- **Suggested Itineraries:** We offer tailored itineraries based on the duration of your stay, highlighting must-see attractions as well as off-the-beaten-path locations to ensure a comprehensive experience.
- **Insider Insights:** Keep an eye out for insider tips from locals and seasoned travelers that will deepen your understanding of the city and its culture, helping you discover the true essence of Innsbruck.
- **Maps and Resources:** The guide includes maps and additional resources to support your journey, making it easy to plan your routes and explore the city with confidence.

Innsbruck: A Snapshot

As the capital of the Austrian state of Tyrol, Innsbruck is a city of striking contrasts, known for its historical significance as well as its contemporary, cosmopolitan atmosphere. Having hosted the Winter Olympics twice, the city continues to draw athletes and tourists from across the globe.

- **Historical Riches:** Innsbruck's history reaches back to Roman times, but its medieval and Baroque architecture are particularly captivating. Notable historical sites include the Hofburg Imperial Palace, the famous Golden Roof, and the grand Court Church.
- **Natural Beauty:** Surrounded by the majestic Alps, Innsbruck is an outdoor enthusiast's dream. Activities such as hiking, skiing, and mountaineering attract adventurers to the area. The Nordkette mountain range, accessible via a modern cable car, offers breathtaking vistas and exhilarating experiences.
- **Cultural Vibrancy:** Innsbruck boasts a lively cultural scene with numerous museums, galleries, and theaters. The Tyrolean Folk Art Museum and the Grassmayr Bell Foundry are just a couple of the many venues where visitors can explore local heritage and craftsmanship.
- **Educational Hub:** Innsbruck is home to the University of Innsbruck, making it a center for education and innovation. The student population contributes to a dynamic and youthful atmosphere, supporting a diverse array of cultural events and festivals year-round.

Top 10 Innsbruck Experiences

1. **Explore the Old Town:** Stroll through the narrow streets of Altstadt, where history is brought to life with charming shops, cafes, and architectural wonders like the Golden Roof and City Tower.

2. **Visit the Imperial Palace:** Uncover the splendor of the Hofburg, a magnificent example of Habsburg architecture, and delve into the lives of Austrian royalty.

3. **Ski the Alps:** Take advantage of Innsbruck's proximity to premier ski resorts, offering slopes suitable for all skill levels amidst breathtaking alpine scenery.

4. **Ride the Nordkette Cable Car:** Climb to the summit of the Nordkette mountain range for sweeping views of the city and the chance to hike or ski.

5. **Experience Tyrolean Culture:** Immerse yourself in local traditions at the Tyrolean Folk Art Museum or enjoy a traditional music and dance performance.

6. **Visit Ambras Castle:** Discover this Renaissance castle, which houses an intriguing collection of art and armor, alongside beautifully landscaped gardens.

7. **Enjoy the Views from the Hungerburg Funicular:** This modern funicular offers stunning views as it transports you from the city center to the mountains in minutes.

8. **Discover the Swarovski Crystal Worlds:** Just outside Innsbruck, this enchanting attraction features dazzling crystal art installations and a captivating garden.

9. **Relax in the Hofgarten:** Wander through the tranquil Imperial Gardens, an ideal spot for relaxation and a taste of nature in the city's heart.

10. **Savor Local Cuisine:** Enjoy Tyrolean culinary specialties at traditional inns and restaurants, sampling dishes such as Wiener Schnitzel, Tiroler Gröstl, and Apfelstrudel.

Trip Planner: When to Go and How Long to Stay

When to Go

- **Spring (March to May):** Spring is a lovely time to visit Innsbruck as the weather becomes warmer and flowers begin to bloom. It's an ideal season for outdoor activities like hiking and sightseeing, with fewer tourists compared to summer.
- **Summer (June to August):** Summer is the peak tourist season, featuring long days and numerous cultural events. It's perfect for exploring the city, hiking, and attending open-air concerts, but expect larger crowds and higher accommodation rates.
- **Autumn (September to November):** Fall is a beautiful time in Innsbruck, with vibrant foliage and cooler temperatures. It's a great season for hiking and cultural festivals, with fewer visitors than in summer.
- **Winter (December to February):** Innsbruck becomes a winter wonderland, drawing ski enthusiasts and holiday travelers. The city is lively with Christmas markets, and the nearby ski resorts are in full operation.

How Long to Stay

- **Short Visit (2-3 Days):** Concentrate on the highlights, including the Old Town, Hofburg, and a trip up the Nordkette. A quick day trip to Ambras Castle or the Swarovski Crystal Worlds can also be fit in.
- **Extended Stay (4-6 Days):** Dive deeper into the city's cultural offerings and natural beauty. Explore more neighborhoods, enjoy a day or two of skiing, and visit nearby villages such as Hall in Tirol.
- **Week-Long Adventure (7+ Days):** Fully experience the region's offerings with multiple day trips, outdoor excursions, and thorough exploration of Innsbruck's museums and cultural sites. Leave time for relaxation and absorbing the alpine atmosphere.

Innsbruck effortlessly combines its rich historical appeal with the excitement of outdoor adventures. Use this guide to fully immerse yourself in everything this remarkable destination has to offer, and prepare for an unforgettable journey through the heart of the Alps.

Getting to Know Innsbruck

Innsbruck is the capital city of Tyrol, a region in western Austria, known for its stunning location amid the Alps. This city uniquely combines history, culture, and natural beauty, making it an attractive destination for visitors seeking a rich and diverse experience. From its medieval Old Town to its grand Baroque architecture and lively cultural scene, Innsbruck has a wealth of attractions that invite exploration and enjoyment. This chapter provides a deep dive into what makes Innsbruck special, including its historical roots, cultural landscape, architectural wonders, and the traditions and people that define its unique character.

A Brief History of Innsbruck

Early Beginnings

Innsbruck has a history that stretches back over a thousand years, with its beginnings rooted in ancient Roman times. The area now called Innsbruck was first settled by the Rhaetian people, a Celtic tribe, before the Romans expanded their empire into the region around 15 BC. The Romans established a military outpost called Veldidena, which is now part of the suburb of Wilten. This location was strategically important because it allowed the Romans to control the Brenner Pass, a critical Alpine crossing that connected northern and southern Europe.

As the Roman Empire declined, control of the region shifted to Bavarian and Lombard rulers during the Early Middle Ages. The town of Innsbruck itself began to take shape in the late 12th century when the Counts of Andechs founded a market settlement at the crossing of the Inn River. This crossing gave the town its name, "Innsbruck," which means "bridge over the Inn."

Growth and Prosperity in the Middle Ages

Innsbruck quickly became a key center for trade because of its strategic position along the route through the Alps. The construction of the Inn Bridge, first mentioned in historical records in 1187, helped facilitate commerce, and the settlement grew in importance. By 1239, Innsbruck had been granted city rights, and in 1363, the powerful Habsburg family took control of the city, marking the beginning of a long period of growth and significance.

Under Habsburg rule, Innsbruck flourished as a center of administration and culture. In 1420, Duke Frederick IV, also known as "Frederick of the Empty Pockets," made Innsbruck the capital of Tyrol. This move attracted artisans, traders, and scholars, creating a vibrant community. The city's prosperity was further boosted by its role as a stopping point for traders and pilgrims traveling across the Alps.

The Renaissance and Baroque Influence

The Renaissance period was a golden age for Innsbruck, as it became a center of art and learning. Emperor Maximilian I, who ruled from 1490 to 1519, played a major role in transforming Innsbruck into a city of architectural and cultural grandeur. He commissioned many projects, including the famous Golden Roof (Goldenes Dachl), a lavish balcony decorated with 2,657 gold-plated copper tiles to celebrate his wedding and symbolize his power.

In the 16th and 17th centuries, Innsbruck continued to thrive, embracing Baroque architecture and culture. The construction of the Hofkirche and the Hofburg Imperial Palace highlighted the city's importance as a seat of power. The Hofkirche is home to the elaborate cenotaph of Emperor Maximilian I, surrounded by 28 life-sized bronze statues of historical figures.

Modern Development and the 20th Century

The 19th and 20th centuries brought industrialization and modernization to Innsbruck. The city expanded beyond its medieval walls, with new neighborhoods and infrastructure developments. The arrival of the railway in 1858 further enhanced Innsbruck's role as a transportation hub, facilitating trade and tourism.

In the 20th century, Innsbruck gained international recognition by hosting the Winter Olympics twice, first in 1964 and again in 1976. These events brought global attention to Innsbruck, showcasing its natural beauty and winter sports facilities. The city continued to grow and diversify, embracing modernity while preserving its historical heritage.

The Cultural Landscape

A City of Festivals and Events

Innsbruck's cultural scene is as varied and lively as its history. The city hosts numerous festivals and events throughout the year, celebrating everything from music and dance to food and art. These events showcase the city's cultural richness and give visitors a chance to experience its energetic spirit.

One of the most popular festivals is the Innsbruck Festival of Early Music, held every August. This festival brings together renowned musicians and ensembles from around the world to perform works from the Renaissance and Baroque periods. Concerts are held in various historic venues, providing a magical backdrop for the performances.

The Tyrolean Festival Erl, held in the nearby village of Erl, is another cultural highlight. This summer festival features opera and classical music performances in a striking modern venue set against the stunning alpine landscape. It attracts music lovers and performers from across the globe.

In winter, Innsbruck transforms into a magical wonderland with its traditional Christmas markets. The Old Town market, with its festive stalls, twinkling lights, and seasonal treats, captures the essence of an Austrian Christmas. Visitors can enjoy mulled wine, roasted chestnuts, and handcrafted gifts while soaking in the holiday atmosphere.

Museums and Galleries

Innsbruck is home to a wealth of museums and galleries that reflect its rich cultural heritage. The Tyrolean State Museum (Ferdinandeum) is one of the city's most important cultural institutions. It houses an extensive collection of art, historical artifacts, and natural history exhibits, providing insight into the region's history and culture.

For art enthusiasts, the Galerie im Taxispalais offers a platform for contemporary art, featuring exhibitions by both local and international artists. The gallery's dynamic program includes a diverse range of media, from painting and sculpture to photography and video installations.

Tyrolean State Museum

Address: Universitätsstraße 2, 6020 Innsbruck, Austria

Phone: +43 512 584 400

Website: https://www.tiroler-landesmuseum.at/en/

The Grassmayr Bell Foundry and Museum is another unique cultural attraction. As one of the oldest bell foundries in Europe, it offers a fascinating glimpse into the art and craft of bell-making. Visitors can learn about the history of bells, witness the casting process, and explore the museum's collection of bells from around the world.

Grassmayr Bell Foundry and Museum

Address: Grassmayrstraße 1, 6020 Innsbruck, Austria

Phone: +43 512 581 931

Website: https://www.grassmayr.com/en/

Innsbruck's Unique Architecture

A Blend of Styles

Innsbruck's architecture is a testament to its rich history and diverse influences. The city's buildings reflect a harmonious blend of architectural styles, from medieval and Renaissance to Baroque and modern. This eclectic mix creates a unique urban landscape that captivates visitors.

The Old Town, or Altstadt, is a treasure trove of medieval and Renaissance architecture. Narrow cobblestone streets are lined with colorful facades, ornate doorways, and charming arcades. The Golden Roof, with its shimmering tiles, is a standout feature that draws the eye and embodies the city's historical significance.

Baroque Grandeur

The Baroque period left an indelible mark on Innsbruck's architectural landscape. The Hofburg Imperial Palace is a prime example of Baroque architecture, with its elegant facades, opulent interiors, and beautifully landscaped gardens. The palace was once the residence of Tyrolean rulers and Habsburg emperors, and today it serves as a museum and cultural venue.

The Court Church (Hofkirche) is another architectural masterpiece from the Baroque era. Its striking interior features the impressive cenotaph of Emperor Maximilian I, surrounded by larger-than-life bronze statues. The church's design and craftsmanship are a testament to the artistic and architectural achievements of the time.

Court Church (Hofkirche)

Address: Hofkirche Innsbruck, Universitätsstraße 2, 6020 Innsbruck, Austria

Contact Information:

- **Phone:** +43 512 59489
- **Email:** hofkirche@tiroler-landesmuseen.at

Modern Innovations

Innsbruck's architectural evolution continues with modern and innovative designs that complement its historical heritage. The Bergisel Ski Jump, designed by renowned architect Zaha Hadid, is a striking example of contemporary architecture. The structure's sleek lines and futuristic design have made it an iconic landmark, offering panoramic views of the city and surrounding mountains.

Bergisel Ski Jump

The Hungerburg Funicular, also designed by Zaha Hadid, showcases modern engineering and design. The funicular's stations feature dynamic shapes and translucent materials, creating a seamless connection between the city and the mountains.

Hungerburg Funicular

- Location/Address: Rennweg 3, 6020 Innsbruck, Austria

- Timings: Varies throughout the year, typically 7:15 AM to 7:15 PM.

- Price range varies

Innsbruck's commitment to blending tradition with innovation is evident in its urban development projects, which prioritize sustainability and environmental consciousness. The city's architecture reflects a forward-thinking approach while honoring its historical roots.

The People and Traditions of Tyrol

A Proud Heritage

The people of Innsbruck and Tyrol take great pride in their heritage, which is deeply rooted in Alpine traditions and customs. Tyroleans are known for their hospitality, warmth, and strong sense of community, making visitors feel welcome and at home.

Traditional Tyrolean clothing, such as the dirndl for women and lederhosen for men, is often worn during festivals and cultural events. These garments are a symbol of regional identity and are cherished for their craftsmanship and historical significance.

Festivals and Celebrations

Festivals and celebrations play a central role in Tyrolean life, providing an opportunity for communities to come together and celebrate their traditions. The Almabtrieb, or cattle drive, is a particularly important event in rural areas. It marks the end of summer when cattle are brought down from the alpine pastures to the valleys. The cattle are adorned with colorful flowers and bells, and the event is celebrated with music, dancing, and feasting.

The Tyrolean Fasnacht, or carnival, is another vibrant tradition that brings communities together. This pre-Lenten festival features elaborate masks, costumes, and processions, with each village putting its own unique spin on the celebrations. Fest is a time for merriment and revelry, reflecting the region's rich cultural heritage.

Culinary Traditions

Tyrolean cuisine is an integral part of the region's cultural identity, with hearty and flavorful dishes that reflect the Alpine environment. Traditional meals are often based on locally sourced ingredients, such as potatoes, dairy products, and meats.

Popular dishes include Tiroler Gröstl, a hearty pan-fried dish of potatoes, onions, and meat, often topped with a fried egg. Kaiserschmarrn, a sweet pancake dish served with fruit compote, is a favorite dessert enjoyed by locals and visitors alike.

Tyrolean hospitality extends to the dining experience, with traditional inns and restaurants offering a warm and welcoming atmosphere. Sharing a meal is an opportunity to connect with the local culture and savor the flavors of the region.

Language and Identity

The primary language spoken in Innsbruck and Tyrol is German, with a distinct Tyrolean dialect that adds to the region's cultural richness. This dialect is a source of pride for the locals and is often used in everyday conversations.

The Tyrolean identity is closely tied to the land and the mountains, with deep respect for nature and a commitment to preserving the region's traditions. This connection to the land is reflected in the strong sense of community and the emphasis on sustainable living.

Planning Your Trip to Innsbruck

When preparing for a trip to Innsbruck, it's important to think about several details, from what to pack to the best way to get there. Located in the beautiful Austrian Alps, Innsbruck combines the charm of a city with stunning natural surroundings. Whether you're interested in history, culture, or outdoor adventures, planning well can help you enjoy your visit to the fullest. This chapter offers practical advice on preparing for your trip, including tips on transportation and staying connected.

Travel Smart: Tips for the savvy traveler

Research and Planning

The foundation of a great trip is careful research and planning. Before traveling to Innsbruck, learn about the city's attractions, local customs, and travel logistics. Use guidebooks, travel websites, and apps to gather information on popular sights, events, and hidden gems.

- **Understand the Destination:** Learn about Innsbruck's history, culture, and geography to appreciate the city more fully. Get to know different areas, like the charming Old Town and the lively university district, each offering a unique experience.
- **Stay Updated:** Check local news and event calendars for festivals, public holidays, or events during your visit. This helps you plan activities and avoid unexpected changes.
- **Create an itinerary:** Make a flexible schedule that includes must-see spots but leaves room for spontaneity. Allow time for exploring and relaxing, and be open to finding new places off the typical tourist path.

Budgeting Your Trip

Setting a realistic budget is key to enjoying a stress-free vacation. Innsbruck can be experienced on various budgets, from luxury stays to more affordable options.

- **Accommodation:** Choose where to stay based on your budget and preferences. Innsbruck has everything from luxury hotels to cozy guesthouses, budget hostels, and vacation rentals.
- **Dining:** Plan for food costs, balancing restaurant meals with local market snacks. Innsbruck is famous for its food, offering traditional Tyrolean dishes and international cuisine.
- **Transportation:** Plan your travel costs, including flights, trains, and local transportation. Consider buying transport passes or tickets in advance to save money.
- **Attractions and Activities:** Research the entry fees for museums, attractions, and activities you want to try. Look for discounts or city passes that can save you money by bundling different experiences.

Travel Insurance

Getting travel insurance is a smart move to protect yourself from unexpected issues. Insurance can cover medical emergencies, trip cancellations, or lost luggage.

- **Coverage:** Pick a policy that covers medical costs, trip cancellations, and your belongings. Make sure it includes activities you plan to do, like skiing or hiking.
- **Policy Details:** Read the policy carefully to understand what is included. Keep a copy of your insurance documents with you during your trip.

Health and Safety

Taking steps to protect your health and safety is important while traveling.

- **Health precautions:** talk to your doctor about recommended vaccines or health advice for Austria. Bring a basic first-aid kit with bandages, painkillers, and any prescription medicines you need.
- **Safety Tips:** Innsbruck is generally safe, but it's always good to be careful. Keep your belongings secure, especially in crowded places, and be aware of your surroundings.

Cultural Etiquette

Understanding local customs and etiquette can make your trip more enjoyable and help you connect with locals.

- **Language:** German is the official language in Innsbruck, but many people speak English, especially in tourist areas. Learning a few simple German phrases can be appreciated and make interactions more rewarding.
- **Dress Code:** Dress according to the season and planned activities. Austrians often dress smartly, so consider wearing slightly nicer clothes for dining out or attending events.
- **Respect Local Customs:** Be aware of cultural norms, like greeting people with "Grüß Gott" and showing respect in religious or historic sites.

Packing and preparation

Packing wisely can greatly improve your travel experience. Bringing the right essentials ensures comfort and convenience during your trip.

Seasonal Packing Tips

Innsbruck's weather changes with the seasons, so pack appropriately to stay comfortable.

- **Winter (December to February):** Winters can be cold and snowy, especially in the mountains. Pack warm clothes like thermal layers, a heavy coat, hats, gloves, and waterproof boots. Rent ski equipment locally to save space.
- **Spring (March to May):** Spring weather can be unpredictable, with mild temperatures and occasional rain. Pack layers, including a waterproof jacket, sweaters, and durable walking shoes.
- **Summer (June to August):** Summers are warm and ideal for outdoor activities. Pack light clothes, sunscreen, a hat, and comfortable hiking shoes for exploring trails.
- **Autumn (September to November):** Fall brings cooler weather and colorful leaves. Pack layers, including a warm jacket and scarf, and sturdy shoes for hiking.

Essential Travel Items

In addition to clothes, some items are essential for a smooth and enjoyable trip to Innsbruck.

- **Travel Documents:** Make sure you have a valid passport, visa (if needed), and other important documents. Keep copies of them in a separate place.
- **Travel Adapters:** Austria uses Type F electrical outlets with a 230V standard voltage. Bring a universal travel adapter to charge your devices.

- **Reusable Water Bottle:** Stay hydrated by carrying a reusable water bottle. Innsbruck's tap water is safe to drink.
- **Daypack:** Bring a lightweight backpack for day trips. It should fit essentials like snacks, a map, and a camera.

Packing Tips for Active Travelers

If you plan to do outdoor activities, pack appropriately for comfort and safety.

- **Outdoor Gear:** Bring gear suitable for hiking, skiing, or other activities, like moisture-wicking clothes, sunglasses, and a hat.
- **Footwear:** Get comfortable shoes suitable for walking and outdoor activities. Break in new shoes before your trip to avoid blisters.
- **Safety Equipment:** If skiing or snowboarding, consider renting helmets and other safety gear locally for proper fit and compliance with local rules.

Getting There: Flights and Trains

Innsbruck is well-connected by air and rail, making it accessible from major cities in Europe and beyond. Choosing the right transportation can enhance your trip.

Flights to Innsbruck

Flying is a convenient way to reach Innsbruck, especially from distant places.

- **Innsbruck Airport (INN):** Located 4 kilometers from the city center, Innsbruck Airport has direct flights from various European cities, especially in winter. Airlines like Austrian Airlines, Lufthansa, and EasyJet serve this airport.
- **Vienna International Airport (VIE):** For international travelers, Vienna International Airport offers more flights. From Vienna, you can reach Innsbruck by train or domestic flight.
- **Munich Airport (MUC):** Another major international airport near Innsbruck is Munich Airport. It's a scenic 2-hour train ride to Innsbruck from Munich, making it popular with travelers.

Train Travel to Innsbruck

Traveling by train is a scenic and relaxing way to reach Innsbruck, letting you enjoy the stunning alpine landscapes.

- **Austrian Railways (ÖBB):** Austria's rail network connects Innsbruck with major cities in Austria and nearby countries. Trains are frequent, comfortable, and offer amazing views of the Alps.
- **EuroCity (EC) Trains:** EuroCity trains connect Innsbruck with cities like Munich, Zurich, and Verona, offering high comfort and onboard amenities.
- **Booking Tickets:** Buy train tickets ahead of time to get the best prices and seat options. Use the ÖBB or Deutsche Bahn websites for booking and current schedules.

Navigating Innsbruck: Public Transport and Biking

Once in Innsbruck, getting around is easy with the city's efficient public transport system and bike-friendly setup.

Public Transport

Innsbruck's public transport is reliable and affordable, making it simple to explore the city and nearby areas.

- **Trams and Buses:** Operated by Innsbrucker Verkehrsbetriebe (IVB), the tram and bus network covers the city. Trams are convenient for city travel, while buses connect Innsbruck with nearby towns.
- **Tickets and Passes:** Buy single tickets or day passes from machines, kiosks, or the IVB app. Consider a 24-hour or 72-hour pass for unlimited travel in the city.
- **Regional Buses and Trains:** For trips outside Innsbruck, regional buses and trains provide easy connections to places like Swarovski Crystal Worlds and ski resorts.

Biking in Innsbruck

Cycling is a popular and eco-friendly way to explore Innsbruck, with its extensive bike paths and rental services.

- **Bike Rentals:** Innsbruck has several bike rental shops offering hourly or daily rentals. Electric bikes are also available for extra assistance.
- **Bike Paths:** The city has many bike paths for exploring neighborhoods and scenic areas. The Inn Valley Cycling Trail is a favorite for longer rides.
- **Safety Tips:** Always wear a helmet and follow traffic rules when biking. Watch out for tram tracks and pedestrian zones, and use bike lanes when possible.

Staying Connected: Wi-Fi and Local SIM Cards

Staying connected while traveling is important for navigation, communication, and accessing travel info. Innsbruck provides several ways to stay connected.

Wi-Fi Access

Wi-Fi is widely available in Innsbruck, making it easy to use the internet on the go.

- **Hotels and Accommodations:** Most places to stay in Innsbruck offer free Wi-Fi. Check with your hotel for login details.

- **Cafés and Restaurants:** Many cafes and restaurants have free Wi-Fi for customers. Look for Wi-Fi signs or ask staff for the network name and password.
- **Public Wi-Fi:** Innsbruck offers free public Wi-Fi in some areas, like the Old Town and public squares. Connect to the "Innsbruck Public" network for access.

Local SIM Cards

For constant connectivity, buying a local SIM card is convenient and cost-effective.

- **Mobile providers:** Major providers in Austria include A1, T-Mobile, and Drei. Buy SIM cards at airports, train stations, and phone shops in the city.
- **Prepaid Plans:** Choose a prepaid plan that fits your data and call needs. Many plans offer unlimited data and local calls, perfect for short visits.
- **Activation:** SIM cards can usually be activated right away. Follow the instructions or ask staff for help if needed.

Roaming Options

If you don't want a local SIM card, check with your provider about international roaming options.

- **Roaming Packages:** Many providers offer packages that let you use your existing plan abroad, including data, calls, and texts.
- **Wi-Fi Calling:** Use Wi-Fi calling apps like WhatsApp or Skype to make calls and send messages over Wi-Fi without roaming charges.

WHERE TO STAY IN INNSBRUCK

Innsbruck, the charming capital of Tyrol, Austria, is not only known for its stunning alpine views and rich history but also for its wide range of accommodations to suit every type of traveler. Whether you're seeking luxury, comfort, budget-friendly options, or unique stays with a touch of local character, Innsbruck offers it all. This chapter provides an extensive guide on where to stay in Innsbruck, highlighting the best neighborhoods and accommodations to ensure a memorable experience.

Best Neighborhoods for Every Traveler

Altstadt (Old Town)

Street of Altstadt

Overview: Altstadt, or the Old Town, is the historical heart of Innsbruck. It's where you'll find the city's most iconic landmarks, such as the Golden Roof, St. Anne's Column, and the Imperial Palace. This area is perfect for those who want to be immersed in history and enjoy the convenience of having attractions, shops, and restaurants just steps away.

Why Stay Here: Staying in Altstadt means you're in the midst of Innsbruck's rich cultural heritage. The narrow cobblestone streets and medieval architecture create a unique and charming atmosphere.

MAP OF ALTSTADT

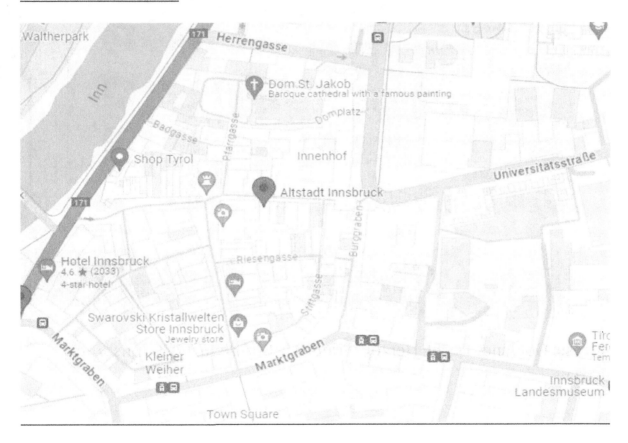

Address: Altstadt Innsbruck, Herzog-Friedrich-Straße, 6020 Innsbruck, Austria.

Herzog-Friedrich-Straße is one of the main streets running through the Old Town, where many of the key landmarks, such as the Golden Roof (Goldenes Dachl), the City Tower (Stadtturm), and the Helblinghaus, are located. The Old

Town is a pedestrian-friendly area filled with narrow, cobblestone streets, medieval buildings, shops, cafes, and historical sites.

Highlights:

- **Golden Roof (Goldenes Dachl):** A symbol of Innsbruck, this golden-tiled roof is a must-see.

Address: Goldenes Dachl, Herzog-Friedrich-Straße 15, 6020 Innsbruck, Austria.

- **Hofburg Imperial Palace:** A beautiful example of Baroque architecture with stunning interiors.

Address: Hofburg Innsbruck, Rennweg 1, 6020 Innsbruck, Austria.

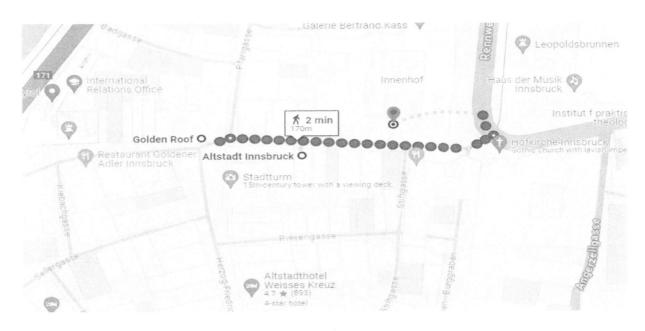

Walk Path from Golden Roof to Hofburg

- **City Tower (Stadtturm):** Offers panoramic views of the city and the surrounding mountains.

Address: Stadtturm Innsbruck, Herzog-Friedrich-Straße 21, 6020 Innsbruck, Austria.

Saggen

Address: Saggen District, 6020 Innsbruck, Austria.

MAP OF SAGGEN

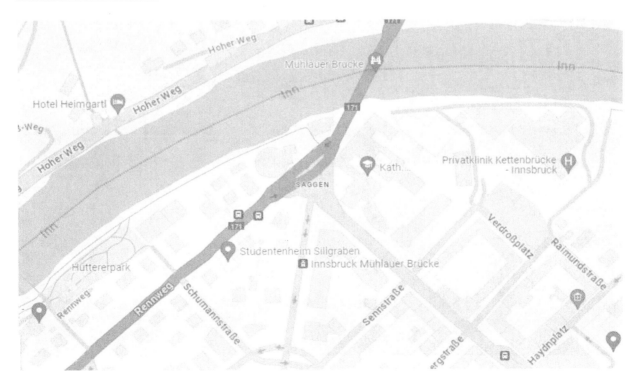

Overview: Saggen is a quiet, upscale residential neighborhood just north of the Old Town. Known for its elegant villas and leafy streets, Saggen provides a tranquil setting with easy access to the city center.

Why Stay Here: If you're looking for a peaceful stay while still being close to the action, Saggen is an ideal choice. It's perfect for families and those seeking a more laid-back atmosphere.

Highlights:

- **Tyrolean State Museum (Tiroler Landesmuseum):** showcases art and history from the region.
- **Innsbruck's Botanical Garden:** A serene spot for nature lovers.
- **Access to the Inn River:** Enjoy walking or biking along the river paths.

Wilten

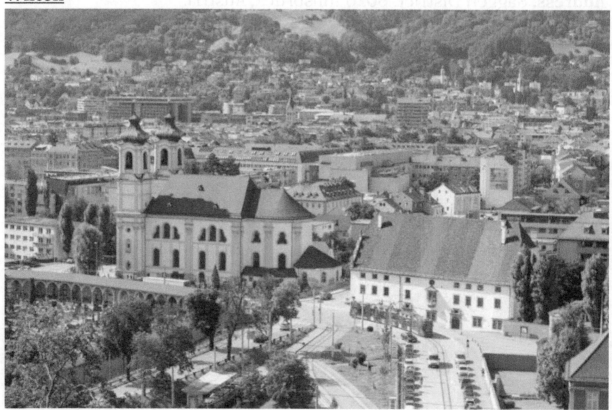

Overview: Located south of the Old Town, Wilten is a vibrant neighborhood known for its artistic vibe and historical sites. It's home to the Basilica of Wilten and the Triumphal Arch, adding to its cultural appeal.

Why Stay Here: Wilten is great for those who appreciate art and history, offering a mix of local life and tourist attractions. It's also close to the main train station, making it convenient for travelers.

Highlights:

- **Basilica of Wilten:** A stunning Baroque church with a rich history.

Walk Path to the Baroque church

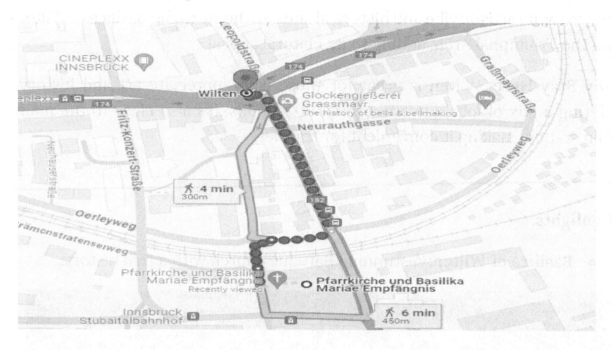

Pradl

MAP OF PRADL

Address: Pradl District, 6020 Innsbruck, Austria

Overview: Pradl is a lively and diverse neighborhood located east of the city center. It's a hub for shopping and local dining, with a mix of modern and traditional elements.

Why Stay Here: If you're interested in experiencing Innsbruck's local life and enjoying a variety of dining and shopping options, Pradl is a great choice. It's also well connected to public transport.

Highlights:

- **Sillpark Shopping Center:** One of the largest shopping malls in Innsbruck.
- **Rapoldi Park:** A green oasis perfect for a leisurely stroll or picnic.
- **Olympiaworld Innsbruck:** A sports complex offering various activities.

Hötting

Overview: Hötting is a residential area located on the western hillside, offering breathtaking views of Innsbruck and the surrounding mountains. It's ideal for nature lovers and those who enjoy outdoor activities.

Why Stay Here: Stay in Hötting if you're looking for a peaceful retreat with easy access to hiking trails and nature. It's perfect for those who want to combine city life with outdoor adventures.

Highlights:

- **Höttinger Alm:** A popular hiking destination with stunning views.
- **Panoramaweg:** A scenic walking path offering panoramic vistas.
- **Botanic Garden of the University of Innsbruck:** Features a diverse range of plants.

Luxury Hotels

Hotel Schwarzer Adler

Location: Kaiserjägerstraße 2, Innsbruck

Overview: This five-star hotel combines modern luxury with historic charm. Located close to the Old Town, Hotel Schwarzer Adler offers elegant rooms, a rooftop terrace with stunning views, and a renowned restaurant.

Highlights:

- **Spa and Wellness Area:** Relax with a range of treatments and facilities.
- **Restaurant Neuwirt:** Offers gourmet Tyrolean and international cuisine.
- **Historical Architecture:** Experience the blend of history and modern comfort.

The Penz Hotel

Location: Adolf-Pichler-Platz 3, Innsbruck

Overview: The Penz Hotel is a modern luxury hotel in the heart of Innsbruck, known for its sleek design and exceptional service. The hotel features a rooftop bar with panoramic views of the city and the Alps.

Highlights:

- **Rooftop Bar:** Enjoy cocktails with a view at The 5th Floor.
- **Contemporary Rooms:** Stylishly designed with comfort in mind.
- **Central Location:** Perfect for exploring Innsbruck's attractions.

Grand Hotel Europa

Location: Südtiroler Platz 2, Innsbruck

Overview: Combining traditional elegance with modern amenities, Grand Hotel Europa offers a luxurious stay in a prime location. It's close to the train station and within walking distance of the Old Town.

Highlights:

- **Europa Stüberl Restaurant:** Serves exquisite Tyrolean and international dishes.
- **Historic Rooms:** Experience the grandeur of the past with modern comforts.
- **Fitness and Sauna:** Facilities to relax and rejuvenate.

NALA Individuellhotel

Location: Müllerstraße 15, Innsbruck

Overview: This unique boutique hotel offers individually designed rooms, each with its own character and charm. Located near the city center, NALA Individuellhotel is perfect for those seeking a personalized experience.

Highlights:

- **Creative Design:** Each room is a work of art, offering a unique experience.
- **Garden Lounge:** Relax in the hotel's serene garden area.
- **Eco-Friendly Initiatives:** Committed to sustainable practices.

Mid-Range Comforts

Hotel Innsbruck

Location: Innrain 3, Innsbruck

Overview: Situated along the Inn River, Hotel Innsbruck offers comfortable accommodations with easy access to the Old Town. The hotel features a wellness area with a pool, sauna, and steam room.

Highlights:

- **River Views:** Enjoy picturesque views of the Inn River.
- **Wellness Facilities:** Relax after a day of exploring with spa amenities.
- **Proximity to Attractions:** Conveniently located near major sights.

Stage 12 Hotel by Penz

Location: Maria-Theresien-Straße 12, Innsbruck

Overview: Stage 12 Hotel offers modern comfort in a central location. With its contemporary design and amenities, this hotel is ideal for travelers seeking convenience and style.

Highlights:

- **City Views:** Many rooms offer stunning views of the cityscape.
- **Fitness Center:** Stay active with a range of equipment and facilities.
- **Bar and Lounge:** Enjoy drinks and snacks in a chic setting.

Hotel Mondschein

Location: Mariahilfstraße 6, Innsbruck

Overview: Hotel Mondschein is a family-run hotel located near the Inn River, offering comfortable accommodations with a touch of traditional Tyrolean hospitality.

Highlights:

- **Cozy Atmosphere:** Enjoy a warm and welcoming environment.
- **Historic Building:** Experience the charm of a 15th-century building.
- **Breakfast Buffet:** Start your day with a delicious spread of local specialties.

AC Hotel Innsbruck

Location: Salurner Straße 15, Innsbruck

Overview: This Marriott property offers a modern and stylish stay with a range of amenities. It's conveniently located near the main train station and Olympiaworld Innsbruck.

Highlights:

- **Fitness Center:** Equipped with the latest machines for a good workout.
- **AC Lounge:** Relax with a drink or snack in a contemporary setting.
- **Spacious Rooms:** Designed for comfort and convenience.

Budget-Friendly Options

Hostel Marmota

Location: Tummelplatzweg 2, Innsbruck

Overview: Hostel Marmota offers budget-friendly accommodations with a relaxed atmosphere. It's located in a quiet area near the Ambras Castle, providing easy access to both nature and the city center.

Highlights:

- **Affordable Rates:** Ideal for budget-conscious travelers.
- **Social Atmosphere:** Meet fellow travelers in the common areas.
- **Garden Area:** Enjoy the outdoor space for relaxation and socializing.

Youth Hostel Innsbruck

Location: Reichenauerstraße 147, Innsbruck

Overview: This well-equipped youth hostel provides basic accommodations at an affordable price. It's located near the Olympic Village, offering a range of activities for guests.

Highlights:

- **Budget Accommodations:** Perfect for solo travelers and groups.
- **Communal Kitchen:** Prepare your own meals to save on dining costs.
- **Recreational Facilities:** Access to sports fields and activities.

Montagu Bed & Beers

Location: Mariahilfstraße 22, Innsbruck

Overview: Montagu Bed & Beers is a unique and affordable option that combines hostel accommodations with a lively pub atmosphere. It's located along the Inn River, close to the Old Town.

Highlights:

- **Bar and Lounge:** Enjoy craft beers and socialize with locals and travelers.
- **Cozy Rooms:** Comfortable dormitory and private rooms available.
- **River Views:** Scenic location along the Inn River.

Pension Stoi

Location: Salurner Straße 7, Innsbruck

Overview: Pension Stoi offers simple and affordable accommodations in a central location. It's a family-run guesthouse that provides a friendly and welcoming environment.

Highlights:

- **Central Location:** Close to the main train station and city center.
- **Basic Comforts:** Clean and comfortable rooms at a reasonable price.
- **Personalized Service:** Friendly staff and personalized attention.

Mapping Out Your Stay in Innsbruck

Innsbruck is a city that seamlessly blends its historical charm with modern amenities, offering a wide range of accommodations to suit every traveler's needs. Whether you're looking for luxury, comfort, budget-friendly options, or unique stays with character, Innsbruck has something for everyone. By choosing the right neighborhood and accommodation, you'll ensure a memorable and enjoyable stay in this alpine gem.

Mapping Highlights:

1. **Altstadt (Old Town):** For history enthusiasts and those seeking central locations.
   - **Key Accommodations:** Hotel Schwarzer Adler, Hotel Innsbruck, Weisses Rössl.
2. **Saggen:** For a peaceful and upscale experience.

- **Key Accommodations:** Grand Hotel Europa, NALA Individuellhotel.

3. **Wilten:** For a vibrant and artistic atmosphere.
   - **Key Accommodations:** The Penz Hotel, Stage 12 Hotel by Penz.

4. **Pradl:** For a local and lively experience with shopping and dining.
   - **Key Accommodations:** Hotel Mondschein, AC Hotel Innsbruck.

5. **Hötting:** For nature lovers and those seeking stunning views.
   - **Key Accommodations:** Gasthof Olberg, Pension Paula.

Continuing our exploration of Innsbruck's remarkable sights, we move to Maria-Theresien-Strasse and its surroundings, where history and modernity meet, offering visitors a fascinating mix of cultural and architectural wonders. This bustling area is known for its vibrant atmosphere, shopping opportunities, and significant landmarks. Additionally, Innsbruck's natural beauty can be appreciated in its green spaces and panoramic views. Here's an in-depth look at these attractions and how they contribute to Innsbruck's unique charm.

Maria-Theresien-Strasse and Surroundings

Triumphal Arch (Triumphpforte)

Overview

The Triumphal Arch is one of Innsbruck's most iconic landmarks, standing proudly at the southern end of Maria-Theresien-Strasse. Erected in 1765, this monumental arch was commissioned by Empress Maria Theresa to commemorate the marriage of her son, Archduke Leopold, to the Spanish princess Maria Luisa. The arch also serves as a memorial to the death of her husband, Emperor Francis I.

Address: Triumphpforte, Maria-Theresien-Straße, 6020 Innsbruck, Austria.

Architectural Features

- **Rococo Design:** The Triumphal Arch is a fine example of Rococo architecture, characterized by its ornate details, elaborate sculptures, and symmetrical design. The arch is adorned with intricate reliefs and decorative elements that celebrate both the joyous occasion of the marriage and the solemn remembrance of Emperor Francis I.
- **Dual Themes:** The southern façade of the arch is dedicated to the wedding celebration, featuring festive decorations and allegorical figures representing joy and prosperity. The northern façade, in contrast, is a tribute to the late emperor, with symbols of mourning and remembrance.

Cultural Significance

The Triumphal Arch stands as a testament to Innsbruck's historical and cultural heritage, reflecting the city's role as a center of power during the Habsburg era. It serves as a gateway to Maria-Theresien-Strasse, inviting visitors to explore the vibrant heart of Innsbruck.

St. Anne's Column (Annasäule)

- **Baroque Style:** The column is a striking example of Baroque architecture, featuring a tall marble shaft topped with a statue of St. Anne, the patron saint of Tyrol. The base of the column is adorned with statues of other saints, including St. George, St. Cassian, St. Vigilius, and St. Anne's daughter, the Virgin Mary.
- **Decorative Elements:** The column is embellished with intricate carvings and decorative details that reflect the artistic trends of the Baroque period. The surrounding area is a popular gathering spot for locals and tourists alike.

Cultural Significance

St. Anne's Column is not only a historical monument but also a symbol of Tyrolean identity and pride. It serves as a focal point on Maria-Theresien-Strasse, offering visitors a place to pause and reflect on the region's rich history.

The Tyrolean State Museum (Ferdinandeum)

include Gothic sculptures, Renaissance paintings, Baroque masterpieces, and contemporary art.

- **Historical Artifacts:** The museum's historical exhibits feature artifacts from the Roman era, the Middle Ages, and the Habsburg period, providing insights into the region's rich and diverse history.
- **Natural History:** The Ferdinandeum also boasts a comprehensive natural history collection, showcasing the flora, fauna, and geological features of Tyrol.

Cultural Significance

The Tyrolean State Museum is a hub of cultural and educational activity, offering visitors a deeper understanding of Tyrol's heritage. Its diverse exhibits and programs cater to all ages, making it a must-visit destination for those interested in art, history, and science.

Modern Innsbruck

The Innsbruck Nordkette Cable Car

Overview

The Innsbruck Nordkette Cable Car is a popular attraction that offers visitors a unique opportunity to experience the natural beauty of the Alps. The cable car connects Innsbruck with the Nordkette mountain range, providing easy access to hiking trails, ski slopes, and breathtaking vistas.

Location on the Map

Key Features

- **Modern Engineering**: The Nordkette Cable Car is a feat of modern engineering, featuring state-of-the-art cabins that offer a comfortable and scenic ride. The journey begins in the city center and ascends to the top of the mountain range in just a few minutes.
- **Spectacular Views**: The cable car offers stunning views of Innsbruck, the Inn Valley, and the surrounding peaks. The journey is a visual feast, with each stop providing a different perspective of the landscape.

Activities and Attractions

- **Hiking and Skiing**: The Nordkette offers a variety of outdoor activities for all seasons, including hiking, skiing, and snowboarding. The area is known for its challenging slopes and well-marked trails.

- **Alpine Zoo:** Located halfway up the mountain, the Alpine Zoo is home to a diverse range of animals native to the Alps, including bears, wolves, and lynxes. It's a great stop for families and nature enthusiasts.

Tirol Panorama Museum

Location on the map

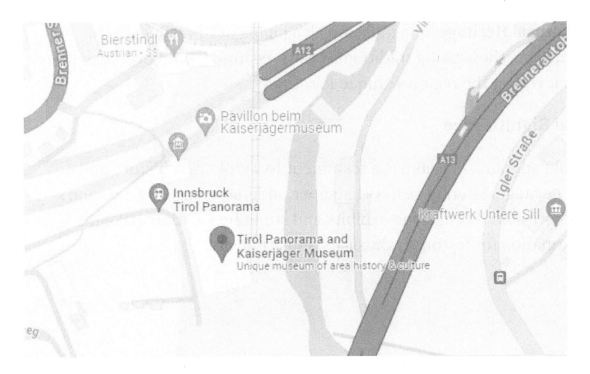

Address: Tirol Panorama Museum, Bergisel 1-2, 6020 Innsbruck, Austria

Overview

The Tirol Panorama Museum is a cultural attraction that offers visitors a unique insight into the history and culture of Tyrol. Located on the Bergisel plateau, the museum is home to the famous Giant Panoramic Painting, a 360-degree depiction of the Tyrolean struggle for freedom.

Exhibits and collections

- **Giant Panoramic Painting:** The centerpiece of the museum is the Giant Panoramic Painting, which depicts the 1809 Tyrolean Rebellion against Bavarian and Napoleonic forces. The painting is a masterpiece of 19th-century art, offering a vivid portrayal of a pivotal moment in Tyrolean history.
- **Military History:** The museum's exhibits explore Tyrol's military history, featuring artifacts, weapons, and uniforms from various periods. Visitors can learn about the region's strategic importance and its role in shaping European history.

- **Cultural Heritage:** The museum also highlights Tyrol's cultural heritage, showcasing traditional crafts, costumes, and everyday objects that reflect the region's unique identity.

Cultural Significance

The Tirol Panorama Museum is a testament to Tyrol's rich history and cultural heritage, offering visitors a deeper understanding of the region's past and present. Its engaging exhibits and stunning location make it a must-visit destination for history enthusiasts and art lovers.

Green spaces and scenic views

Hofgarten

Address: Hofgarten Innsbruck, Kaiserjägerstraße, 6020 Innsbruck, Austria.

Overview

The Hofgarten is a historic park located near the center of Innsbruck, offering a peaceful retreat from the hustle and bustle of the city. With its beautifully landscaped gardens, tranquil ponds, and shady pathways, the Hofgarten is a favorite spot for locals and visitors alike.

Key Features

- **Historic Gardens:** The Hofgarten has a long and storied history, dating back to the 15th century. The gardens have been redesigned several times over the centuries, reflecting various styles and influences.
- **Floral Displays:** The park is known for its vibrant floral displays, featuring a wide variety of plants and flowers that change with the seasons.
- **Recreational Activities:** The Hofgarten offers a range of recreational activities, including walking paths, a playground, and a chessboard area. It's a great place for a leisurely stroll or a family outing.

Cultural Significance

The Hofgarten is a symbol of Innsbruck's commitment to preserving its natural beauty and providing green spaces for its residents and visitors. It offers a tranquil oasis in the heart of the city, inviting people to relax and enjoy the natural surroundings.

Botanical Gardens

- **Greenhouses:** The gardens feature several greenhouses that house tropical and subtropical plants, providing a warm and humid environment for species that thrive in such conditions.
- **Educational Programs:** The Botanical Gardens offer a range of educational programs and workshops for visitors of all ages, focusing on topics such as plant conservation, biodiversity, and sustainable gardening.

Cultural Significance

The Botanical Gardens are a testament to Innsbruck's commitment to environmental education and conservation. They offer a space for learning and discovery, inspiring visitors to appreciate and protect the natural world.

Ambras Castle and Gardens

Address: Ambras Castle (Schloss Ambras), Schlossstraße 20, 6020 Innsbruck, Austria.

Overview

Ambras Castle is a Renaissance gem located on a hill overlooking Innsbruck. The castle is renowned for its stunning architecture, fascinating history, and beautifully landscaped gardens. It is a must-visit destination for anyone interested in art, history, and nature.

Historical Background

Ambras Castle was built in the 16th century by Archduke Ferdinand II as a residence for his morganatic wife, Philippine Welser. The castle is famous for its art collections and was one of the first museums in the world.

Architectural Features

- **Renaissance Design:** The castle is a masterpiece of Renaissance architecture, featuring elegant facades, decorative elements, and harmonious proportions. Its design reflects the artistic trends of the period and the personal tastes of its patrons.

- **Art Collections**: Ambras Castle is home to an extensive collection of art and artifacts, including portraits, armor, and curiosities. The Spanish Hall, with its magnificent ceiling frescoes, is one of the highlights of the castle's interior.

Gardens and Grounds

- **Landscaped Gardens**: The gardens of Ambras Castle are a testament to the art of Renaissance landscaping, featuring carefully manicured lawns, ornamental flowerbeds, and charming pathways. The gardens offer a tranquil setting for a leisurely stroll and provide stunning views of the surrounding mountains.
- **Cultural Events**: The castle and its gardens host a variety of cultural events throughout the year, including concerts, exhibitions, and theatrical performances. These events offer visitors a chance to experience the cultural richness of Innsbruck in a historic and picturesque setting.

Cultural Significance

Ambras Castle is a symbol of Innsbruck's artistic and cultural heritage, reflecting the city's role as a center of art and learning during the Renaissance period. Its collections and gardens offer a glimpse into the opulent lifestyle of the Habsburgs and the artistic achievements of the time.

Day Trips and Excursions from Innsbruck

Innsbruck, nestled in the heart of the Austrian Alps, is not only a vibrant city with a rich cultural and historical heritage but also an ideal starting point for exploring some of Tyrol's most stunning natural landscapes and nearby attractions. The region offers a variety of day trips and excursions that cater to adventurers, history buffs, art enthusiasts, and nature lovers alike. This chapter will guide you through some of the most exciting destinations around Innsbruck, including the majestic Nordkette Mountain Range, the charming village of Seefeld in Tirol, the mesmerizing Swarovski Crystal Worlds, the historic town of Kufstein with its imposing fortress, and the quaint Hall in Tirol.

Nordkette Mountain Range

Overview

The Nordkette Mountain Range serves as a stunning backdrop to Innsbruck and offers a vast playground for outdoor enthusiasts. Located just a short distance from the city, the Nordkette is part of the Karwendel Alps and features breathtaking peaks, panoramic views, and a variety of recreational activities. This area is easily accessible via a modern cable car system that transports visitors from the heart of Innsbruck to the top of the mountains in a matter of minutes.

Hiking and Skiing

The Nordkette Mountain Range is renowned for its excellent hiking trails and skiing opportunities, making it a year-round destination for outdoor activities.

- **Hiking:** In the warmer months, the Nordkette offers an extensive network of hiking trails suitable for all skill levels. From leisurely walks to challenging hikes, the trails provide stunning views of the surrounding Alps and the Inn Valley below. Popular hikes include the Goetheweg, which offers panoramic vistas and connects to the famous Karwendelhaus mountain hut.
- **Skiing:** During the winter, the Nordkette transforms into a ski paradise with a range of slopes and runs catering to skiers and snowboarders. The area is known for its challenging terrain, including the Hafelekar Run, one of Europe's steepest ski slopes. For those seeking a more relaxed experience, there are also gentle slopes suitable for beginners and families.

CABLE CAR ADVENTURES

The Innsbruck Nordkette Cable Car is a marvel of modern engineering that provides easy access to the mountain range, offering breathtaking views along the way. The journey begins at the Hungerburg Funicular, located in the city center, and continues with the cable car ride to Seegrube and Hafelekar.

- **Hungerburg Funicular:** Designed by the renowned architect Zaha Hadid, the funicular features a sleek, futuristic design and offers a smooth ride from the city center to the Hungerburg district.
- **Seegrube Station:** At an altitude of 1,905 meters, Seegrube offers stunning views of Innsbruck and the surrounding peaks. Visitors can enjoy a meal at the Panorama Restaurant, which serves traditional Tyrolean dishes with a modern twist.
- **Hafelekar Station:** The final stop on the cable car journey, Hafelekar is located at 2,334 meters above sea level. From here, visitors can take in panoramic views of the Alps and explore the surrounding trails.

Map and Location

- **Location:** The Nordkette Mountain Range is located just north of Innsbruck, accessible via the Innsbruck Nordkette Cable Car.
- **Starting Point:** Hungerburg Funicular Station, located in the city center.

Seefeld in Tirol

Overview

Seefeld in Tirol is a picturesque alpine village located just a short train ride from Innsbruck. Known for its pristine natural beauty and year-round recreational activities, Seefeld is a popular destination for both winter sports enthusiasts and summer hikers. The village is situated on a sunny plateau at an elevation of 1,200 meters, offering a serene and scenic escape from the hustle and bustle of city life.

Winter Sports and Summer Hikes

Seefeld is renowned for its world-class winter sports facilities and scenic hiking trails, making it a destination for outdoor activities in every season.

- **Winter Sports:** Seefeld is a paradise for winter sports enthusiasts, offering a variety of activities such as cross-country skiing, downhill skiing, snowboarding, and ice skating. The village has hosted the Winter Olympics twice and is home to some of the best cross-country skiing trails in the world.
- **Summer Hikes:** In the summer, Seefeld transforms into a hiker's paradise with a network of well-marked trails that cater to all levels of experience. Popular hikes include the Wildmoos Plateau, which offers panoramic views of the surrounding mountains and lush meadows.

Scenic Train Ride

One of the highlights of a visit to Seefeld is the scenic train ride from Innsbruck, which offers breathtaking views of the Tyrolean landscape. The journey takes approximately 30 minutes and traverses picturesque valleys, dense forests, and towering peaks, providing a memorable experience for travelers.

- **Location:** Seefeld in Tirol is located approximately 25 kilometers northwest of Innsbruck, accessible by train from Innsbruck Hauptbahnhof.
- **Starting Point:** Innsbruck Hauptbahnhof (main train station).

Swarovski Crystal Worlds

Address: Swarovski Crystal Worlds, Kristallweltenstraße 1, 6112 Wattens, Austria.

Overview

Swarovski Crystal Worlds, located in the village of Wattens near Innsbruck, is a dazzling attraction that combines art, nature, and shopping in a unique and immersive experience. Created by the famous crystal company Swarovski, this enchanting destination features stunning art installations, a lush garden, and a shopping area offering a wide range of crystal products.

Art Installations and Shopping

- **Art Installations:** Swarovski Crystal Worlds is home to a series of captivating art installations created by renowned artists from around the world. The installations are housed within the Chambers of Wonder, a series of rooms that showcase the beauty and versatility of crystal in various forms.
- **Crystal Cloud:** One of the most iconic installations is the Crystal Cloud, which consists of over 800,000 hand-mounted crystals that shimmer and sparkle in the sunlight. The installation is set in a tranquil garden, providing a magical and serene setting for visitors.
- **Shopping:** The Swarovski Crystal Worlds Store offers a wide range of crystal products, from jewelry and accessories to home decor and collectibles. Visitors can browse the extensive selection and find unique gifts and souvenirs.

Location: Swarovski Crystal Worlds is located in Wattens, approximately 20 kilometers east of Innsbruck.

Starting Point: accessible by car or shuttle bus from Innsbruck Hauptbahnhof.

Kufstein and Its Fortress

- **Kufstein Fortress:** The Kufstein Fortress is a medieval castle that dates back to the 13th century. The fortress has played a significant role in the region's history, serving as a strategic stronghold and a symbol of power. Today, it is a popular tourist attraction, offering guided tours, interactive exhibits, and stunning views.
- **Castle Museum:** The fortress houses a museum that provides insights into the history and architecture of the castle, as well as the cultural heritage of the region. Visitors can explore the museum's exhibits, which include historical artifacts, weapons, and artworks.
- **Fortress Concerts:** Kufstein Fortress is renowned for its open-air concerts and events, which take place in the castle's courtyard and attract visitors from near and far. The concerts feature a diverse range of musical genres, from classical to contemporary, and offer a unique and memorable experience.

Local Culinary Delights

Kufstein is also known for its culinary offerings, with a variety of restaurants and cafes serving traditional Tyrolean dishes and international cuisine. Visitors can enjoy local specialties such as Tiroler Gröstl, dumplings, and schnitzel, accompanied by a selection of regional wines and beers.

- **Location:** Kufstein is located approximately 70 kilometers northeast of Innsbruck, accessible by car or train.
- **Starting Point:** Innsbruck Hauptbahnhof (main train station) for train travel.

Hall in Tirol

Map of Hall in Tirol

Overview

Hall in Tirol is a picturesque medieval town located just a short distance from Innsbruck. Known for its well-preserved old town and rich history, Hall in Tirol offers visitors a glimpse into its past as a thriving center of commerce and culture. The town is home to a variety of historical landmarks, charming streets, and cultural attractions.

Historic Town Center

The heart of Hall in Tirol is its historic town center, characterized by its narrow cobblestone streets, colorful facades, and beautiful architecture. Visitors can explore the town's charming squares, browse local shops, and enjoy the vibrant atmosphere.

- **Hasegg Castle:** A prominent landmark in Hall in Tirol, Hasegg Castle is a medieval fortress that dates back to the 13th century. The castle has played a significant role in the town's history and is home to the Mint Museum, which showcases the history of coin minting in the region.

Mint Museum

The Mint Museum in Hasegg Castle is a fascinating attraction that offers insights into the history of coin minting and the economic importance of Hall in Tirol. The museum features interactive exhibits, historical artifacts, and guided tours that provide a deeper understanding of the minting process and its impact on the region's development.

- **Mint Tower:** Visitors can climb the Mint Tower for panoramic views of the town and the surrounding landscape. The tower offers a unique perspective on the town's history and architecture, making it a must-visit destination for history enthusiasts.

Location: Hall in Tirol is located approximately 10 kilometers east of Innsbruck, accessible by car or train.

Innsbruck's Culture and Art

Innsbruck, the capital city of Tyrol in western Austria, is a captivating blend of tradition and modernity, nestled in the heart of the Alps. Known for its stunning mountain scenery, Innsbruck is also a cultural hub, offering a rich tapestry of art, history, and music. The city's cultural scene is vibrant and diverse, with institutions and events that reflect both its historical roots and contemporary influences. This exploration of Innsbruck's culture and art delves into four key aspects: the Tyrolean Folk Art Museum, the Grassmayr Bell Foundry, contemporary art spaces, and the city's music and performance scene, including its theaters and concert halls.

The Tyrolean Folk Art Museum

The Tyrolean Folk Art Museum (Tiroler Volkskunstmuseum) is one of the most significant museums dedicated to regional culture in Austria. Located next to the Hofkirche in the historic center of Innsbruck, the museum is housed in a 17th-century former monastery that itself is a remarkable architectural landmark. The museum offers an extensive collection of artifacts that provide insight into the traditional life and culture of Tyrol.

Collections and Exhibitions

The Tyrolean Folk Art Museum boasts an impressive collection of artifacts, ranging from traditional costumes and textiles to tools, furniture, and religious folk art. These items are displayed in a way that highlights the craftsmanship and artistry of Tyrolean artisans over the centuries. The museum's exhibits are organized thematically, allowing visitors to explore different aspects of rural life, including farming, domestic life, and religious practices.

One of the museum's highlights is its collection of traditional Tyrolean costumes, which reflect the diversity of the region's cultural heritage. These costumes, often worn during festivals and religious ceremonies, are characterized by intricate embroidery and vivid colors. The museum also showcases a collection of masks used in traditional Tyrolean parades and festivals, offering insight into the region's unique customs and celebrations.

The museum's rooms are also furnished with examples of traditional Tyrolean parlors, complete with wood-paneled walls and ceilings, intricately carved furniture, and hand-painted chests. These recreations provide a glimpse into the living conditions and aesthetic preferences of Tyrolean families in the past.

Cultural Significance

The Tyrolean Folk Art Museum plays a crucial role in preserving and promoting Tyrolean cultural heritage. It serves as a repository of knowledge about traditional ways of life that have been passed down through generations. By showcasing the region's folk art and customs, the museum helps to keep these traditions alive in a rapidly changing world.

In addition to its permanent collections, the museum hosts temporary exhibitions and events that explore contemporary interpretations of Tyrolean culture. These initiatives help to bridge the gap between past and present, engaging visitors with the living traditions of the region.

The Grassmayr Bell Foundry

The Grassmayr Bell Foundry, located just a short distance from Innsbruck's city center, is one of the oldest family-run businesses in Austria and a remarkable example of traditional craftsmanship. Founded in 1599, the foundry has been producing bells for over 400 years, making it a significant part of Innsbruck's industrial and cultural heritage.

History and Craftsmanship

The Grassmayr Bell Foundry has been passed down through 14 generations of the Grassmayr family, each contributing to the refinement and perfection of the bell-making process. The foundry's long history is a testament to the family's dedication to their craft and the enduring importance of bells in both religious and secular contexts.

The process of making a bell at the Grassmayr Foundry is a complex and labor-intensive endeavor. It begins with the creation of a mold, which is meticulously crafted to ensure the bell's precise shape and size. The molten bronze is then poured into the mold, a process that requires skill and precision to avoid imperfections. Once the bell has cooled and hardened, it is tuned to achieve the desired sound, a task that requires an acute ear and expert knowledge.

The Bell Museum

Adjacent to the working foundry is the Grassmayr Bell Museum, which offers visitors a fascinating glimpse into the art and science of bell-making. The museum features interactive exhibits that explain the technical aspects of bell production, including acoustics and metallurgy. Visitors can also see historical examples of bells produced by the foundry, each with its own unique story and significance.

The museum's exhibits are designed to be engaging and educational, appealing to visitors of all ages. Through hands-on activities and multimedia presentations, visitors can learn about the history of bells, their role in society, and the craftsmanship that goes into creating them.

Cultural Impact

Bells have played a significant role in the cultural and religious life of communities throughout history. They mark important events, call people to worship, and serve as symbols of celebration and remembrance. The Grassmayr Bell Foundry continues to produce bells for churches, schools, and public institutions around the world, ensuring that this age-old tradition remains alive and relevant.

The foundry's commitment to quality and innovation has earned it a reputation as one of the leading bell producers globally. By maintaining traditional techniques while embracing modern technology, the Grassmayr

Bell Foundry exemplifies the harmonious blend of history and progress that characterizes Innsbruck's cultural landscape.

Contemporary Art Spaces

Innsbruck is home to a vibrant contemporary art scene, with numerous galleries and spaces dedicated to showcasing the work of both established and emerging artists. These venues provide a platform for creative expression and experimentation, reflecting the dynamic and evolving nature of contemporary art.

Galerie im Taxispalais

One of Innsbruck's premier contemporary art spaces is the Galerie im Taxispalais. Housed in a historic building that dates back to the 17th century, the gallery offers a striking contrast between its classical architecture and the cutting-edge art it exhibits. The Galerie im Taxispalais features a diverse range of contemporary artworks, including painting, sculpture, photography, video, and installation art.

The gallery is known for its innovative and thought-provoking exhibitions, which often address pressing social and political issues. By engaging with contemporary themes and ideas, the Galerie im Taxispalais fosters dialogue and critical reflection among artists and audiences alike.

Kunstraum Innsbruck

Another important venue for contemporary art in Innsbruck is Kunstraum Innsbruck. This independent, artist-run space is dedicated to promoting experimental and interdisciplinary art practices. Kunstraum Innsbruck hosts a wide range of exhibitions, performances, and events, providing a platform for both local and international artists to showcase their work.

Kunstraum Innsbruck is committed to pushing the boundaries of artistic expression, encouraging artists to take risks and explore new ideas. The space's experimental approach has made it a hub for innovation and creativity, attracting artists and audiences who are eager to engage with the latest developments in contemporary art.

Art Biennials and Festivals

In addition to its permanent art spaces, Innsbruck hosts several art biennials and festivals that celebrate contemporary art and culture. These events bring together artists, curators, and art enthusiasts from around the world, transforming the city into a vibrant center of creativity and exchange.

One such event is the Innsbruck Biennial, which features a diverse program of exhibitions, performances, and discussions. The biennial provides a platform for exploring contemporary art practices and ideas, fostering collaboration and dialogue among artists and audiences.

The Role of Contemporary Art in Innsbruck

Contemporary art plays a vital role in Innsbruck's cultural landscape, offering new perspectives and challenging conventional ways of thinking. By embracing innovation and experimentation, the city's contemporary art spaces contribute to a dynamic and evolving cultural scene that reflects the diversity and complexity of modern life.

Innsbruck's commitment to contemporary art is also evident in its support for public art projects and initiatives. These projects often involve collaborations between artists and local communities, creating artworks that engage with the city's public spaces and environment. By integrating art into everyday life, Innsbruck demonstrates its dedication to fostering a culture of creativity and innovation.

Music and Performance: Innsbruck's Theaters and Concert Halls

Innsbruck has a rich musical tradition, with a vibrant performing arts scene that encompasses a wide range of genres and styles. The city is home to several theaters and concert halls that host performances by both local and international artists, offering audiences a diverse array of musical and theatrical experiences.

Tiroler Landestheater Innsbruck

The Tiroler Landestheater Innsbruck is the city's premier venue for opera, theater, and ballet. Located in the heart of Innsbruck, the theater is a stunning example of neo-Baroque architecture, with an ornate façade and elegantly appointed interiors.

The Tiroler Landestheater hosts a varied program of performances, including classical operas, contemporary plays, and innovative dance productions. The theater's commitment to artistic excellence is evident in its collaborations with renowned directors, conductors, and choreographers from around the world.

In addition to its mainstage productions, the Tiroler Landestheater also offers a range of educational and outreach programs, aimed at engaging new audiences and fostering a love of the performing arts. Through workshops, lectures, and interactive events, the theater seeks to inspire and educate audiences of all ages.

Innsbruck Festival of Early Music

The Innsbruck Festival of Early Music (Innsbrucker Festwochen der Alten Musik) is a highlight of the city's cultural calendar. Held annually in the summer, the festival celebrates the rich tradition of early music, with performances of works from the medieval, Renaissance, and Baroque periods.

The festival attracts renowned musicians and ensembles from around the world, who perform in some of Innsbruck's most beautiful historic venues, including churches and palaces. The festival's program includes concerts, operas, and recitals, offering audiences a unique opportunity to experience the beauty and complexity of early music.

The Innsbruck Festival of Early Music also plays a crucial role in promoting the study and performance of early music, supporting research and education initiatives that contribute to the preservation and understanding of this important musical tradition.

Haus der Musik

The Haus der Musik is a modern cultural center in Innsbruck, dedicated to music and performing arts. The facility houses several concert halls and rehearsal spaces, providing a state-of-the-art venue for a wide range of performances, from classical concerts to contemporary music and theater.

The Haus der Musik is home to several of Innsbruck's leading musical institutions, including the Tyrolean Symphony Orchestra and the Innsbruck State Conservatory. The center's diverse program of events reflects its commitment to fostering creativity and collaboration across different genres and disciplines.

Jazz and Contemporary Music

In addition to its classical music offerings, Innsbruck has a thriving jazz and contemporary music scene. The city hosts several festivals and events that celebrate these genres, attracting musicians and audiences from around the world.

One notable event is the New Orleans Festival, which brings the vibrant sounds of jazz and blues to Innsbruck's streets and venues. The festival features performances by both local and international artists, offering audiences a chance to experience the energy and excitement of live jazz music.

Innsbruck's commitment to contemporary music is also evident in its support for new and emerging artists. The city's music venues and festivals provide a platform for experimental and avant-garde performances, encouraging innovation and creativity in the musical arts.

Eating and Drinking in Innsbruck

Innsbruck, located in the heart of the Austrian Alps, is a city that not only boasts breathtaking landscapes but also a rich culinary heritage. With a variety of offerings ranging from hearty Tyrolean dishes to elegant fine dining options, Innsbruck provides a culinary journey that caters to a wide range of tastes. This chapter delves into the different aspects of eating and drinking in Innsbruck, guiding you through traditional cuisine, top restaurants, cozy cafés, lively pubs, and bustling food markets.

Traditional Tyrolean Cuisine

Tyrolean cuisine is characterized by its hearty and rustic flavors, reflecting the mountainous region's history and culture. The cuisine primarily focuses on locally sourced, seasonal ingredients, offering a unique taste of the Alpine lifestyle. Here are some of the most iconic dishes you can expect to find:

Key Dishes

1. **Tiroler Gröstl**: A classic Tyrolean dish made with pan-fried potatoes, beef or pork, onions, and spices, usually topped with a fried egg. Often enjoyed as a hearty breakfast or lunch, it epitomizes comfort food in the region.
2. **Käsespätzle**: Soft egg noodles mixed with rich, melted cheese and topped with crispy fried onions. Similar to mac and cheese but with a distinctive Alpine twist, it's a favorite among both locals and visitors.
3. **Speckknödel**: dumplings made from speck (smoked ham), bread, and onions, typically served in a hearty broth or with sauerkraut. Speckknödel showcases the Tyrolean love for incorporating cured meats into their dishes.
4. **Tafelspitz**: A boiled beef dish traditionally served with horseradish, apple sauce, and roasted potatoes. Although it's closely associated with Viennese cuisine, it is also popular in Tyrol and highlights Austria's fondness for meat-focused meals.

5. **Kiachl**: A traditional pastry that is deep-fried and usually enjoyed with either savory or sweet fillings. Kiachl can be filled with sauerkraut or served with lingonberry jam, making it a delicious snack or dessert.

Important Locations for Traditional Cuisine

- **Stiftskeller Innsbruck**: Located in Innsbruck's old town, Stiftskeller offers a traditional setting with a menu full of authentic Tyrolean dishes. The restaurant is housed in a historic building, adding to the dining experience's charm.
- **Gasthof Weisses Rössl**: Known for its cozy atmosphere and history dating back to the 15th century, this inn provides a menu filled with classic Tyrolean and Austrian dishes, including the famous Tiroler Gröstl.
- **Restaurant Sitzwohl**: While offering a modern take on Tyrolean cuisine, Restaurant Sitzwohl respects the region's traditions. It's a great spot to experience innovative dishes that highlight local ingredients.

Top Restaurants for Fine Dining

Innsbruck is home to several fine dining establishments that offer exquisite culinary experiences. These restaurants combine top-quality ingredients with creative presentation and impeccable service, making them ideal for special occasions or sophisticated nights out.

Notable Fine Dining Establishments

1. **Schwarzer Adler Restaurant**: Known for its elegant setting and refined menu, Schwarzer Adler provides an unforgettable dining experience, focusing on regional ingredients to create visually stunning and delicious dishes. The Schwarzer Adler Restaurant is located in Innsbruck, Austria. Specifically, it is part of the Hotel Schwarzer Adler Innsbruck.

2. **Das Schindler**:

Address: Maria-Theresien-Straße 31 6020 Innsbruck, Austria

An upscale restaurant offering a contemporary menu that blends Austrian and international flavors. With an emphasis on seasonal ingredients, Das Schindler provides a dynamic dining experience that evolves with the seasons.

3. **Lichtblick**: Located on the top floor of a modern building, Lichtblick offers panoramic views of the city along with a menu that emphasizes creativity and finesse. It's an ideal spot for a sophisticated meal with a breathtaking backdrop.

Address: Lichtblick Maria-Theresien-Straße 18 Rathausgalerien 7th Floor 6020 Innsbruck, Austria.

4. **Berchtoldshof**: Situated on the outskirts of Innsbruck, this restaurant offers a peaceful setting away from the city's hustle and bustle. The menu features gourmet dishes that highlight the region's flavors, providing a fine dining experience celebrating Tyrolean culture.

Address: Berchtoldshof Schneeburggasse 94 6020 Innsbruck Austria

Important Locations for Fine Dining

- **Sitzwohl**: Renowned for its sophisticated atmosphere and innovative cuisine, Sitzwohl offers a fine dining experience combining local flavors with international influences. The restaurant is known for its attention to detail and excellent wine selection.

Address: Stadtforum 1 6020 Innsbruck, Austria.

- **Restaurant Oniriq**: Chef Christoph Bickel's Restaurant Oniriq offers a unique dining experience that blends creativity and elegance. With a focus on seasonal ingredients, the restaurant's menu changes frequently, ensuring each visit is a new adventure.

Address: Universitätsstraße 5-7 6020 Innsbruck, Austria.

Cozy Cafés and Bakeries

Innsbruck's café culture is a delightful mix of tradition and modernity. Whether you're looking for a quiet place to enjoy a cup of coffee or a lively spot to indulge in delicious pastries, the city has plenty to offer. Cafés and bakeries are an integral part of life in Innsbruck, providing a warm and welcoming atmosphere where people can relax and unwind.

Popular Cafés and Bakeries

1. **Café Sacher Innsbruck**: Known for its world-famous Sachertorte, Café Sacher offers a taste of Viennese coffee culture in the heart of Innsbruck. The elegant setting and rich history make it a must-visit for any traveler.

2. **Konditorei Valier**: This charming bakery is renowned for its delicious cakes, pastries, and chocolates. With a wide selection of sweet treats, Konditorei Valier is a paradise for dessert lovers.

3. **Café Munding**: As one of the oldest cafés in Innsbruck, Café Munding has a long-standing tradition of serving exceptional coffee and pastries. The cozy atmosphere and historic charm make it a favorite among locals and tourists alike.

4. **Café Katzung**: Located in the heart of the old town, Café Katzung offers a welcoming atmosphere and a menu filled with delicious breakfast and brunch options. It's a great spot to start your day or enjoy a leisurely afternoon.

Important Locations for Cafés and Bakeries

- **Bäckerei Ruetz**: With several locations throughout Innsbruck, Bäckerei Ruetz is a popular bakery known for its freshly baked bread and pastries. It's a perfect place to grab a quick breakfast or snack on the go.

- **Strudel-Café Kröll**: Specializing in traditional Austrian strudels, this café offers a wide variety of sweet and savory options. Whether you're craving apple strudel or something more unique, Strudel-Café Kröll is sure to satisfy your taste buds.

Popular Pubs and Breweries

Innsbruck's nightlife scene is vibrant and diverse, with a wide range of pubs and breweries to explore. Whether you're in the mood for a quiet pint or a lively night out, the city's pubs offer a welcoming atmosphere and a great selection of local and international beer.

Notable Pubs and Breweries

1. **Stiftskeller**: Known for its traditional setting and extensive beer selection, Stiftskeller is a popular spot for both locals and tourists. The beer garden provides a perfect place to enjoy a drink and soak in the historic atmosphere.

2. **Tribaun**: A modern craft beer bar, Tribaun offers a rotating selection of local and international craft beers. With its laid-back vibe and knowledgeable staff, it's a great place to discover new and exciting brews.

3. **Bierwirt**: This traditional pub and restaurant offer a wide range of Austrian beers, along with a menu filled with hearty Tyrolean dishes. Bierwirt is a great spot to experience the local beer culture in a cozy setting.

4. **Hofgarten Café**: Located near the beautiful Hofgarten park, this café and bar offer a relaxed atmosphere and a selection of beers and cocktails. It's an ideal spot for unwinding after a day of exploring the city.

Important Locations for Pubs and Breweries

- **The Galway Bay**: A popular Irish pub in Innsbruck, The Galway Bay offers a lively atmosphere, live music, and a wide range of beers and spirits. It's a great place to enjoy a night out with friends and experience a taste of Ireland in the Alps.

- **Weinhaus Happ**: Known for its impressive selection of Austrian wines and beers, Weinhaus Happ provides a sophisticated setting for enjoying a drink and sampling local flavors.

Food Markets and Street Food

Innsbruck's food markets and street food scenes offer a vibrant and diverse culinary experience. From fresh produce to international cuisine, the city's markets are a great place to explore and discover new flavors. Whether you're in the mood for a quick snack or a full meal, Innsbruck's street food vendors provide a delicious and convenient option.

Prominent Food Markets

1. **Markthalle Innsbruck**: This bustling indoor market offers a wide range of fresh produce, meats, cheeses, and baked goods. It's a great place to

experience the local food culture and pick up ingredients for a picnic or home-cooked meal.

2. **Wiltener Platzl Market**: Held every Saturday, this vibrant market features a variety of local vendors selling everything from fresh vegetables to handmade crafts. It's a perfect spot to enjoy a leisurely morning and sample local specialties.

3. **Farmers' Market at Innsbruck Hauptbahnhof**: Located near the main train station, this market offers a convenient location for travelers to explore local products and enjoy a quick bite.

Popular Street Food Options

1. **Bosna**: A popular Austrian street food, Bosna is a spicy sausage served in a toasted bun with onions, mustard, and curry powder. It's a flavorful and satisfying snack that's perfect for enjoying on the go.

2. **Langos**: Originally from Hungary, Langos is a deep-fried flatbread often topped with garlic, cheese, and sour cream. It's a delicious and indulgent treat that can be found at various street food stalls throughout the city.

3. **Pretzels**: These iconic German-style pretzels are a popular snack in Innsbruck, offering a perfect combination of soft, chewy dough and a salty crust. They're a great option for a quick and satisfying bite.

Important Locations for Food Markets and Street Food

- **Maria-Theresien-Straße**: This bustling street in the heart of Innsbruck is home to numerous street food vendors and stalls, offering a wide variety of snacks and meals. It's a great place to explore and experience the city's vibrant street food scene.

- **Innsbruck Christmas Market**: Held annually during the holiday season, the Innsbruck Christmas Market offers a festive atmosphere and a wide range of traditional foods and drinks. From roasted chestnuts to mulled wine, it's a wonderful place to indulge in seasonal treats.

Shopping in Innsbruck

Innsbruck, located in the heart of the Austrian Alps, is a city that seamlessly blends its rich historical heritage with a lively modern culture. Known for its striking architecture, winter sports, and breathtaking landscapes, Innsbruck is also a shopping paradise offering everything from luxury boutiques to local artisan crafts. This chapter explores the diverse shopping experiences available in Innsbruck, highlighting key locations and must-visit spots that cater to a variety of tastes and preferences.

Luxury Boutiques and Department Stores

Innsbruck boasts a range of luxury boutiques and department stores catering to those with discerning tastes. Whether you're in search of high-end fashion, jewelry, or unique accessories, the city's upscale shopping scene is sure to impress.

Maria-Theresien-Straße

Maria-Theresienstraße is one of Innsbruck's most famous shopping streets. This bustling avenue, lined with a mix of modern shops and historic buildings, is home to numerous luxury boutiques and flagship stores. Strolling down this vibrant street, you'll find renowned brands such as Louis Vuitton, Gucci, and Prada, alongside elegant Austrian designers like Lena Hoschek and Swarovski.

Kaufhaus Tyrol.

Kaufhaus Tyrol, a landmark in Innsbruck's shopping scene, is a modern department store located on Maria Theresien-Straße. It offers a wide selection of high-end fashion, beauty products, and home goods, making it a one-stop destination for luxury shopping. The store's sleek architecture and well-curated collections make it a pleasure to explore.

Swarovski Kristallwelten Store Innsbruck

For those enchanted by the brilliance of crystals, the Swarovski Kristallwelten Store in Innsbruck is a must-visit. Located near the Golden Roof, this flagship store showcases Swarovski's exquisite crystal creations, ranging from jewelry and accessories to home decor. The store's stunning displays and innovative designs make it a true gem in Innsbruck's shopping scene.

RathausGalerien
Adjacent to Kaufhaus Tyrol, the Rathaus Galerien is another premier shopping destination. This elegant shopping center features a variety of luxury brands, including Hugo Boss, Max Mara, and Michael Kors. With its sophisticated atmosphere and diverse offerings, the RathausGalerien is a favorite among locals and tourists alike.

Artisan crafts and souvenirs

Innsbruck offers a plethora of shops specializing in artisan crafts and souvenirs for those seeking unique souvenirs and gifts. These establishments provide a glimpse into the region's rich cultural heritage and traditional craftsmanship.

Old Town (Altstadt).

Innsbruck's charming Old Town is a treasure trove of artisan shops and boutiques. Here, visitors can find handcrafted items such as Tyrolean wood carvings, traditional clothing, and intricate lacework. As you stroll through the narrow cobblestone streets, you'll discover hidden gems like family-run stores offering locally made chocolates, preserves, and schnapps.

Spanglergasse
A quaint street in the Old Town, Spanglergasse is known for its artisan workshops and studios. This area is home to skilled craftsmen who create beautiful ceramics, glassware, and textiles. Visitors can watch artisans at work and purchase one-of-a-kind pieces that capture the essence of Tyrolean artistry.

Innsbruck Market Hall (Markthalle Innsbruck)

For a taste of local flavor, Innsbruck Market Hall is a must-visit destination. This bustling market offers a wide range of regional products, from fresh produce and meats to artisanal cheeses and baked goods. It's an ideal place to pick up authentic Tyrolean specialties and sample the region's culinary delights.

Address: Herzog-Siegmund-Ufer 1-3 6020 Innsbruck Austria

Auracher Löchl

Located in the heart of the Old Town, Auracher Löchl is a historic tavern and shop that has been operating for over 600 years. In addition to its renowned restaurant, which serves traditional Tyrolean dishes, Auracher Löchl offers a selection of local products and souvenirs, including schnapps, jams, and traditional clothing.

Address: Römerhofgasse 2-5 6330 Kufstein Austria

Local markets and specialty shops

Innsbruck's local markets and specialty shops provide a delightful shopping experience for those seeking fresh produce, unique ingredients, and gourmet treats. These vibrant markets are integral to the city's culinary scene, offering a wide range of products that reflect the region's agricultural heritage.

Innsbruck Farmers' Market

Held weekly in various locations throughout the city, the Innsbruck Farmers' Market is a popular destination for locals and visitors alike. Here, you can find an array of fresh fruits, vegetables, and herbs, as well as homemade jams, cheeses, and baked goods. The market is an excellent place to sample seasonal produce and interact with local farmers and artisans.

St. Nikolaus District

The St. Nikolaus District, located across the Inn River from the Old Town, is home to a variety of specialty shops and boutiques. This charming neighborhood offers a selection of gourmet food stores, including delicatessens, bakeries, and wine shops. Visitors can explore the district's narrow streets and discover hidden gems offering unique culinary delights and handmade products.

Wilten District

The Wilten District, located south of the city center, is another area known for its specialty shops and markets. The district's vibrant food scene includes artisanal bakeries, organic grocery stores, and specialty coffee shops. Wilten is also home to the Wiltener Wochenmarkt, a weekly market featuring local produce, meats, and crafts.

The Innsbruck Christmas Market

One of the most enchanting shopping experiences in Innsbruck is the annual Christmas Market. Held during the festive season, this market transforms the city's squares into a winter wonderland filled with twinkling lights, festive decorations, and the aroma of mulled wine and roasted chestnuts.

Old Town Christmas Market

The Old Town Christmas Market is the most iconic of Innsbruck's holiday markets. Set against the backdrop of the Golden Roof and surrounded by historic buildings, this market features over 70 stalls offering a wide range of handcrafted gifts, ornaments, and traditional holiday treats. Visitors can enjoy live music, browse the stalls for unique gifts, and savor seasonal delicacies such as gingerbread and marzipan.

Maria-Theresien-Straße Christmas Market

Located in the heart of the city, the Maria-Theresien-Straße Christmas Market offers a more contemporary take on the traditional holiday market. With its modern design and illuminated trees, this market features a mix of international and local vendors offering a variety of gifts, decorations, and culinary delights. The market's central location makes it a convenient stop for holiday shopping and festive entertainment.

Marktplatz Christmas Market

Situated along the banks of the Inn River, the Marktplatz Christmas Market is known for its family-friendly atmosphere and picturesque setting. This market features a range of stalls offering handmade crafts, toys, and holiday treats. Visitors can enjoy a ride on the carousel, explore the petting zoo, and take in the stunning views of the snow-capped mountains.

Innsbruck's festivals and events

Innsbruck, situated in the heart of the Austrian Alps, is a city renowned for its rich cultural events and festivals, offering a blend of tradition and modernity. From the harmonious melodies of early music to the excitement of world-class skiing competitions, Innsbruck's calendar is packed with events that highlight its unique heritage and vibrant atmosphere. This chapter provides an in-depth look at the city's most notable festivals and events, including locations and insights into what makes each occasion special.

The Innsbruck Festival of Early Music

The Innsbruck Festival of Early Music is a prestigious event attracting music enthusiasts from all over the world to celebrate the rich history and artistry of early music. Held annually in July and August, the festival features performances by renowned musicians and ensembles, focusing on music from the Renaissance and Baroque periods.

Venues and Highlights

Ambras Castle

Ambras Castle is one of the main venues for the festival, located just a few kilometers from Innsbruck's city center. The castle's Spanish Hall, known for its excellent acoustics and ornate decorations, provides a magnificent setting. For concerts, visitors can enjoy performances by leading early music artists in this historic venue, enhancing the musical experience with its authenticity and grandeur.

Address: Schlossstraße 20 6020 Innsbruck Austria

Innsbruck's Historic Churches

Several of Innsbruck's historic churches host concerts during the festival. The Court Church (Hofkirche) and the Jesuit Church (Jesuitenkirche) are notable for their stunning architecture and rich history. These sacred spaces offer a serene atmosphere for enjoying choral and instrumental music, providing an intimate connection between the audience and performers.

Christmas markets and winter festivities

Innsbruck's Christmas markets and winter festivities are among the city's most enchanting experiences, transforming the city into a magical winter wonderland. From mid-November to early January, Innsbruck is alive with twinkling lights, festive decorations, and the aromas of seasonal treats, creating a warm and inviting atmosphere for both locals and visitors.

Key Christmas Markets

Old Town Christmas Market

Situated in the heart of Innsbruck's historic Old Town, the Old Town Christmas Market is set against the backdrop of the Golden Roof, a landmark. dating back to the 15th century. The market features over 70 stalls offering handcrafted gifts, ornaments, and traditional holiday treats. Visitors can enjoy live music, browse the stalls for unique gifts, and savor seasonal delicacies such as gingerbread and marzipan. The market's charming setting and festive ambiance make it a must-visit during the holiday season.

Maria-Theresien-Straße Christmas Market

This market, located on Innsbruck's main shopping street, Maria-Theresien-Straße, offers a more contemporary take on the traditional Christmas market. Illuminated trees and modern design elements create a stunning visual display, while a mix of international and local vendors offers a variety of gifts, decorations, and culinary delights. The market's central location makes it a convenient stop for holiday shopping and festive entertainment.

Marktplatz Christmas Market

Located along the banks of the Inn River, the Marktplatz Christmas Market is known for its family-friendly atmosphere and picturesque setting. This market features a range of stalls offering handmade crafts, toys, and holiday treats. Visitors can enjoy a ride on the carousel, explore the petting zoo, and take in the stunning views of the snow-capped mountains. The market's relaxed vibe and scenic location make it a favorite among families and children.

Winter Events and Activities

In addition to the Christmas markets, Innsbruck offers various winter events and activities that celebrate the season. The city hosts several ice skating rinks, including one at the Marktplatz Christmas Market, where visitors can skate while enjoying the festive atmosphere. Innsbruck's Winter Running Festival, held in December, attracts runners of all ages and abilities to participate in races through the city's snow-covered streets.

Alpine Ski World Cup Events

Innsbruck is synonymous with winter sports, hosting several prestigious Alpine Ski World Cup events that draw athletes and spectators from around the globe. These events showcase the region's world-class skiing facilities and provide thrilling entertainment for sports enthusiasts.

Key skiing venues

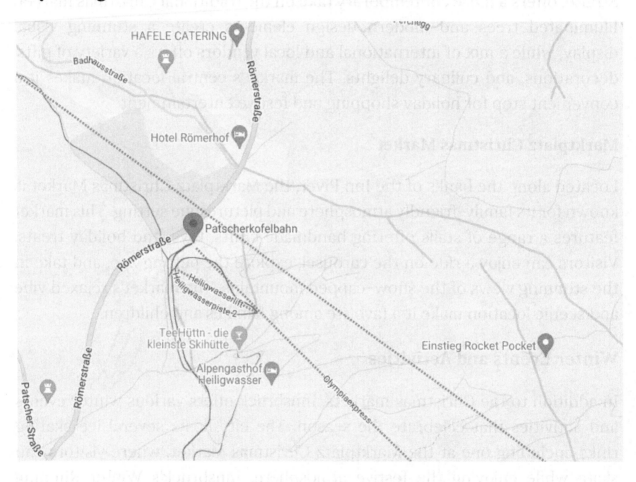

Patscherkofel

Located just south of Innsbruck, Patscherkofel is a historic skiing venue that has hosted numerous World Cup races and Olympic events. The mountain's slopes offer various runs for skiers of all levels, and its state-of-the-art facilities make it a top choice for international competitions. The Patscherkofel World Cup races are a highlight of the skiing season, attracting top athletes and spectators to witness thrilling downhill and slalom competitions. Patscherkofel is a mountain located near Innsbruck, Austria. It is part of the Tux Alps and is a popular destination for skiing, hiking, and other outdoor activities.

Location: Patscherkofel is situated approximately 7 kilometers south of Innsbruck, with the nearest village being Igls, which serves as a base for accessing the mountain. The Patscherkofelbahn cable car provides easy access to the summit from Igls.

Axamer Lizum

Axamer Lizum, located about 19 kilometers from Innsbruck, is another premier skiing destination known for its excellent snow conditions and diverse range of slopes. The resort has hosted several World Cup events and offers a variety of runs for both amateur and professional skiers. The stunning alpine setting and modern amenities make Axamer Lizum a favorite among competitors and visitors.

Address: Axamer Lizum 2 6094 Axams Austria

Nordkette

Accessible from Innsbruck's city center via a cable car, Nordkette offers a unique combination of urban and alpine experiences. The mountain's challenging slopes are a popular choice for advanced skiers and snowboarders, and the Nordkette World Cup events provide a thrilling spectacle for spectators. The resort's proximity to the city makes it an ideal destination for those looking to enjoy world-class skiing and Innsbruck's vibrant nightlife.

Spectator Experience

Attending an Alpine Ski World Cup event in Innsbruck is a memorable experience, offering the chance to witness top athletes compete in breathtaking alpine settings. Visitors can enjoy the excitement of the races while taking in the stunning views of the surrounding mountains. Innsbruck's excellent public transportation system and well-organized event logistics make it easy for visitors to access the ski venues and enjoy the competitions.

Local traditions and seasonal celebrations

Innsbruck's cultural calendar is filled with local traditions and seasonal celebrations that offer a glimpse into the region's rich heritage and community spirit. These events provide an opportunity to experience authentic Tyrolean customs and connect with the local culture.

Key Local Traditions

Fasnacht (Carnival)

Fasnacht, or Carnival, is a vibrant and colorful celebration that takes place in Innsbruck and surrounding Tyrolean villages in the weeks leading up to Lent. The festivities include parades, masked balls, and traditional performances reflecting the region's folklore and customs. The Innsbruck Fasnacht Parade features elaborate costumes and masks, live music, and dance performances, creating a lively and festive atmosphere in the city's streets.

Kirchtag (Church Day)

Kirchtag, or Church Day, is a traditional Tyrolean celebration that combines religious observance with community festivities. The event typically includes a church service, followed by a festive gathering with music, dancing, and local food and drink. Innsbruck's Kirchtag celebrations provide an opportunity to experience the region's hospitality and enjoy traditional Tyrolean cuisine.

Almabtrieb (Cattle Drive)

The Almabtrieb, or cattle drive, marks the end of the summer grazing season when cattle are brought down from the mountain pastures to the valley. The event is celebrated with parades, music, and festive gatherings, as the cattle are adorned with flower garlands and bells. Innsbruck's Almabtrieb festivities offer a unique glimpse into the region's agricultural heritage and are a highlight of the autumn season.

Seasonal Celebrations

Innsbruck's seasonal celebrations offer a diverse range of experiences, from summer music festivals to winter sports competitions. The city's cultural calendar includes events like the Innsbruck Summer Festival, featuring a mix of classical and contemporary music performances, and the Bergsilvester New Year's Eve celebration, which includes fireworks, live music, and a vibrant street party in the city's center.

Practical Information

When planning a visit to Innsbruck, it is essential to consider practical information to ensure a safe and enjoyable trip. This section provides useful tips and resources for navigating the city and making the most of your stay.

Health and Safety Tips

Innsbruck is a safe and welcoming city, but visitors should still take basic precautions to ensure their safety. It is advisable to carry a copy of your passport and important documents, keep valuables secure, and stay informed about local news and events. Travelers should also be aware of their surroundings and avoid isolated areas at night. In case of emergency, the local police, fire, and medical services can be reached by dialing 112.

Money Matters: Currency and Tipping

The currency in Austria is the Euro (€). Credit cards are widely accepted in Innsbruck, but it is advisable to carry some cash for smaller purchases and in case of emergencies. Tipping is customary in Austria, with a typical tip of 5-10% for restaurant service, rounding up the bill for taxis, and leaving small amounts for hotel staff and other services.

Language Basics: Useful German Phrases

While many people in Innsbruck speak English, learning a few basic German phrases can enhance your travel experience and help you connect with locals. Here are some useful phrases:

- **Hello**: Hallo
- **Goodbye**: Auf Wiedersehen
- **Please**: Bitte
- **Thank you**: Danke
- **Yes**: Ja

- **No**: Nein
- **Excuse me**: Entschuldigung
- **How much does this cost?**: Wie viel kostet das?
- **Do you speak English?**: Sprechen Sie Englisch?

Emergency Contacts and Services

In case of emergency, visitors should be aware of the following important contacts and services:

- **Emergency Services (Police, Fire, Ambulance)**: 112
- **Local Police**: 133
- **Fire Department**: 122
- **Ambulance**: 144
- **Innsbruck Tourist Information Center**: +43 512 53560
- **Innsbruck University Hospital**: +43 512 5040

Accessibility Information for Travelers with Disabilities

Innsbruck is committed to providing accessible services and facilities for travelers with disabilities. Many public buildings, museums, and attractions offer wheelchair access, and the city's public transportation system is equipped with low-floor buses and trams. Travelers with specific accessibility needs should contact the Innsbruck Tourist Information Center for detailed information and assistance in planning their visit.

Appendices

The following appendices provide additional resources and suggestions for planning your visit to Innsbruck, including itineraries, maps, and recommended reading.

Suggested Itineraries for 3, 5, and 7 Days

3-Day Itinerary

- **Day 1**: Explore Innsbruck's Old Town, visit the Golden Roof, and enjoy a meal at a traditional Tyrolean restaurant.
- **Day 2**: Take a cable car to the Nordkette mountains for a day of hiking or skiing, and visit the Alpenzoo on the way back.
- **Day 3**: Discover the Ambras Castle and its gardens, and spend the afternoon shopping on Maria-Theresien-Straße.

5-Day Itinerary

- **Days 1-3**: Follow the 3-day itinerary.
- **Day 4**: Visit the Swarovski Kristallwelten in Wattens and explore the nearby town of Hall in Tirol.
- **Day 5**: Take a day trip to the Stubai Valley for hiking or skiing, and relax at the Stubay Leisure Center.

7-Day Itinerary

- **Days 1-5**: Follow the 5-day itinerary.
- **Day 6**: Explore the tztal valley, visit the Aqua Dome thermal spa, and enjoy a scenic drive through the Alps.
- **Day 7**: Visit Innsbruck's museums, such as the Tyrolean State Museum and the Ferdinandeum, and enjoy a farewell dinner at a local restaurant.

Innsbruck maps and walking tours

Innsbruck offers a variety of walking tours that allow visitors to explore the city's history and culture at their own pace. Maps and guides are available at the Innsbruck Tourist Information Center, offering detailed information on walking routes, points of interest, and recommended stops. Popular walking tours include the Innsbruck City Walk, which covers the Old Town and key landmarks, and the River Inn Promenade, which offers scenic views of the city and mountains.

Recommended Reading and Resources

To enhance your understanding and appreciation of Innsbruck and its culture, consider exploring the following recommended reading and resources:

- **"Innsbruck: City and Mountain" by Michael Forcher**: A comprehensive guide to Innsbruck's history, culture, and natural beauty.
- **"The Tyrol: Its People and Culture" by Ralph O'Connor**: An insightful exploration of Tyrolean traditions and customs.
- **Innsbruck Tourist Information Website**: www.innsbruck.info The official website provides up-to-date information on events, attractions, and travel tips.

Made in the USA
Las Vegas, NV
15 December 2024

14314207R00070